Wishes for the Grieving

Poems of Love, Loss and Life After.

Claire Walsh

First Published in the UK in 2023

www.ootb-books.co.uk

ISBN (Paperback) 978-1-7384038-0-6

ISBN (eBook) 978-1-7384038-1-3

Welcome to the book that no-one wants to read. I know I didn't want to write it! Grief hurts and I'm sorry that you are grieving, but we can't change it, so I am on a mission for us to talk more about it, grief, death, dying, all of it. It shouldn't be taboo; it shouldn't be a secret.

We are feeling it, so we should be able to talk about it, to show it and to share it! Also, it's not all doom and gloom. You may not be there yet, or may not ever agree with me, but I can find some positivity in my grief. Grief enables me to find joy in the itchy-scratchy moments of the world. It has allowed me to see the beauty in the wobbles and woes, whereas I once only saw problems.

Now don't get me wrong, this doesn't mean I'm glad I am grieving, or that I suddenly buy into the 'everything happens for a reason' narrative around the person you love dying. But I guess when you have lost love, lost life, lost that special person, nothing else feels so bad. I find myself, when faced with dilemma, trouble, problem, or disaster, thinking 'well at least no one is dead'. I appreciate life, with all its crap, more than I ever did. I don't sweat the small stuff. I accept that life has its ups and downs.

This book is a collection of poetry written throughout my grief journey, a journey that will never end. Grief is not a task to complete. Grief is the experience of the living as they continue to love the people who have died. The pain of my grief means I am alive, and for that I am grateful, it is a privilege denied to many.

Love and Solidarity
Claire

This book is dedicated to everyone who has known the pain of grief, in whatever form.

Remember this is your grief, so do it your way.

Do not let others tell you how or when to grieve.

Your grief, your way, always.

Wishes for the Grieving

I wish you the freedom to grieve your way, and not
let the untouched tell you how to do it.

I wish you the space to scream, shout, laugh, cry,
sing and sob; don't let others silence you.

I wish you the time and space to grieve, without the
uncomfortable trying to move you on.

I wish you the voice to say their name forever, and
the company of those who enjoy hearing it.

I would wish you my perspective without my pain, but
I know that it's too late for that.

So, remember your grief is love, love is good, you are
love and love lasts forever.

The Pain We Call Grief

Heartbreak
doesn't cover it
that pain
that knife in my chest
again
and
again.

Heart held in a vice like grip
squeezed tight
almost to a
STOP.
Racing, then charging,
a proverbial bull in a china shop.

Pain so deep, like nothing before
a deep breath
a slight moment of relief
and then I succumb
to that pain.

That pain we call grief.

My Love Is Dead

My love is dead,
and yet I smile.
Because I held his hand a while.

My love is dead,
and yet I dance.
I know he would, given half a chance.

My love is dead,
and yet I grow.
He wanted me to, that I know.

My love is dead,
and yet I love.
Love is not something you just let go of.

My love is dead,
yet I'm still here.
Here for a reason, that much is clear.

Love is the reason,
the reason for life.
Always and forever his loving wife.

Memories

I wish I could remember every good night kiss.
But memory doesn't work like that.
I wish I could forget death juice.
But memory doesn't work like that.

So many memories that I love to recall.
So many memories that I would give anything to erase.

I remember the first time I saw you.
The twinkle of your eyes and the way my heart fluttered.
My tummy flipped as we talked for the first time.

I remember the last time I saw you.
I held your hand and told you I loved you,
as you took your last breath.
Pain so immense in my chest.
Who knew a broken heart hurt so much.
I have never felt such pain...
and I gave birth to a 10lb 6oz baby!!!

Years move on and I no longer trust my memory.
Is it the menopause or is it grief?
I never want to forget you.

I say your name,
I keep you close,
I will not forget you.

Without You

I'm cold and lost.
Without You.

I'm sad and lonely.
Without You.

Without You.
Who am I?

Without You.
I am not me.

The D Word

Don't say lost or passed away,
Don't say they're gone or sleeping,
Don't wrap it up in cotton wool,
For fear of causing weeping.

I know it will be hard for you,
But be brave, and say instead,
I'm sorry that your husband died.
I'm sorry that he's dead.

Toxic Positivity

Cancer is a cunt.
I can't find the gratitude in that.
I can only find hate, anger, and pain.
I'm lost, I'm hurt, I am bereaved.
How can I be grateful for that?
My heart aches, my eyes leak, my arms yearn.
How can I be grateful for that?
Everything happens for a reason. Bollocks.
You never get more than you can handle. Shite.
Time is the great healer. Like fuck it is.
I cannot be grateful for cancer,
I will never be grateful for his death.
I am not grateful for this pain.
I am grateful for love,
My heart aches because I loved him so.
Thank you, Martin.
I am grateful for happiness,
My eyes leak because we were so happy.
Thank you, Martin.
I am grateful for tenderness,
My arms yearn because they felt such tenderness.
Thank you, Martin.
I cannot be grateful for cancer,
But I am grateful for you.

Shout Out to the Widows

Shouting out to all those wonderful widows out there.

You are strong.

You are smart.

You are beautiful.

You are brave.

This isn't fair.

It hurts like hell.

Do it your way.

It's your grief.

Don't let anyone take that from you.

A Future Lost

I am not just grieving because you have died.
I am not just grieving for times gone by.
I am not just grieving for the here and now.

I am grieving our future lost,
the maybes,
the what ifs,
the I wonders.

The wedding days you will not see,
the changing of our children's lives,
the growing old of you and me
A future lost is what I grieve.

1992-2015

I first saw his eyes in 1992;
I saw them last in 2015,
Those eyes, so kind, so twinkly, so deep,
Just like him.

I first slept in his arms in 1992;
I held his hand as he died in 2015,
Those arms, so strong, so comforting, so warm,
Just like him.

Full of character, charm, and compassion in life,
Bringing heartache, hurt and emptiness in death.

I smile because I was his wife,
I cry because there are no more years left in his life.

Fear

Sometimes fear grips me.
An ice-cold hand around my heart.
The worm in my head telling me,
to love again,
is to grieve again.
I fight the fear
but sometimes it wins.

This is grief.

Old or Dead

We bemoan the aches and pains of aging
The feelings that our health is ailing
Knowing that our eyesight is failing
But it sure beats the alternative!

We hate the wrinkles on our face
Look in the mirror with distaste
Want our hair to stay in place
But it sure beats the alternative!

Saggy tits, weak pelvic floor
We yearn for bodies from before
Chins, one, two, three, four
But it sure beats the alternative!

When thoughts like this are in your head
Remember that you could be dead
Enjoy everyday you have ahead
Being old, or being dead
That's the alternative!

A Fragile Heart

The heart is a fragile thing,
When it's broken, it's broken,
We live with it, we love with it, but it's broken,
It doesn't mean we are broken,
It is quite possible to live with a broken heart,
And to have a good life,
To those people who judge and say 'get over it',
I say I wish you could have my perspective,
Without my pain,
Because I wouldn't wish that on my worst enemy.

The Storm

Wild and windy, wet, and wintery, the storm surrounds me.
Howling in my ears like a screaming banshee.
Hair whipping my face; not controlled like a ringmaster,
Out of control like a toddler in a sweet shop.
Frantic.
Chaotic.
Chaffing my cheeks,
Pin pricks of sand, blasting from the beach.
The storm pushes me.
My weight no match for its strength.
My resilience no match for its punches.
I falter and fall under its power.
I buckle and break.
The storm wins.
Storms have names, personifying them.
This one is mean, nasty, and has a face like thunder.
Its name is Life.

Life with a Broken Heart

You broke my heart.
Yet still I love you.
I miss you.

My heart is still broken.
It has sticking plasters, bandages and glue.
Holding it together.

It still works.
It still beats.
It still loves.

Loves you, loves me, loves others.

And maybe, most importantly, loves life.

Life with a broken heart.

AWAKE!

She is awake again, why can't she sleep?
It escapes her,
Always.
Rambling thoughts around her brain,
Buzzing not zzzzzzzzzzzzzzzing.
Awake again, an absence of sleep,
A missing part of life,
A missing part of her.
No sheep to count.
No pills to pop.
She is awake.
Awake again.
AWAKE!

Sunshine

I am not a sunworshipper,
not by any stretch of the imagination.
I am one of those people who goes an angry shade of red,
followed by milk bottle white.
Factor 50 is my best friend,
and the shade is where I reside.

Yet a sunny day makes me smile.
Blue skies and sunshine give me hope.
A sunny day is filled with promises of happiness,
it's hard to stay sad when the world around you is
light,
bright,
and sunny

The warmth on my skin,
reminds me of a lifetime of tender kisses.
I soak in the sun as I soak in the love,
memories as vivid as the bright sky
and as warm as the midday sun.

I Cried a Loch

Blue skies on a cloudy day
Like a kiss between the tears
Deep water cold and dark
Like a mother's new-born fears

Lush forests, tall and proud
Like the father of the bride
Grey clouds full of rain
Like the lochs that I have cried

The Vase

I am whole and complete as I am.

Yes, there are the cracks and chips that come from life,

from living with a broken heart.

But.

They are part of what makes me whole.

Like rivulets of silver on a china vase, they add to the beauty.

The beauty that is the whole, and complete me.

Magic!

I don't believe in magic
I don't believe in ghosts
If I can't see it - it's not real
That's what puzzles me most

I don't believe in spirits
I don't believe in fate
I only believe in the here and now
I'm so pragmatic
Wait …

I do believe in magic
For I believe in love
I can't see it - yet I feel it
But not from up above

I do believe in magic
I do believe in you
Love in every one of us
That's magic from my point of view

It comes from us
That powerful force
We are love, don't you see
I do believe in magic
The magic is you and me

You!

Remember you are powerful!

Remember you are strong!

Remember you can do it all!

And nothing will go wrong!

From Widow to Wife

I smile when I open my eyes, because I see you.
Sometimes I need to pinch myself to check that it's true.

Your head on the pillow, still a surprise,
I expected it empty after Martin's demise.

A lonely old widow, my predicted life,
Instead, I find, I am your wife.

Looking into your eyes as you rouse from sleep,
I know you feel my love so deep.

A love so deep, so true, so rich,
You stole my heart, you did bewitch.

You cast your spell and I am enchanted,
We are lucky in love,
I won't take that for granted.

Spring Flowers

Bright coloured crowns
Green leaves so deep
Spring flowers on my wedding day
Trumpets of yellow
Cups of pink
Signs of new life, new beginnings
Bulbs that bloom
Year on year
Everlasting
The promise of forever
A wedding day
Till death do us part
20 years of spring flowers
And then
Tulips that wither and die
Petals drop, leaves droop
Daffodils, brown and crisp
Crepe paper flowers
No longer can I feel your touch
Gentle petals on my skin
Bulbs without buds
Emptiness, fears and tears
Without spring flowers

Cliché

His smile.
My heart melted the first time I saw his smile.
Cliché but true.

His eyes twinkled.
His lips curled.
I licked my lips.
Cliché but true.

My stomach flipped.
My cheeks flushed.
He grinned.
Cliché but true.

It was love at first sight.
First smile.
First night.
Cliché but true.

He died.
My heart broke in two.
Cliché but true.
Sometimes only a cliché will do.

My Raison d'Etre

He was my greatest gift,
and my biggest loss.

My happiest moment,
my saddest too.

My reason for laughing,
my reason for crying.

The reason for all that I do.

Now

Now is all we have,
no need to worry or fret,
about the things that haven't come yet.

Now is all we have,
no need to regret,
all those things we wish to forget.

Now is all we have,
stay present, stay here,
enjoy this moment,
live without fear.

Recipe for Kindness

Take a huge dollop of compassion

Add a splash of understanding

Mix with a cupful of generosity

Stir well with patience and tolerance

Sprinkle with love, care, and attention

Bake gently in humanity

And share in copious amounts wherever you go.

Squawking

Goodbye my loving lover.
Goodbye Martin, my man.
Goodbye my dashing darling.
Goodbye my number one fan.

My heart breaks.
Smashing!
Crashing!
I miss you so much.

Tears
Dripping
Slipping
Down my face.
As I yearn for your touch.

Grief
Squawking like an angry bird.
Yowling
Growling
Caterwauling

A raging monster that needs to be heard.

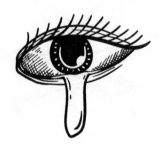

In Conversation with a Widow

"At least they've gone to a better place"

I'll try not to show anger on my face.

"Are you over it yet, it's been a while"

I'll hide my pain behind a smile.

"I'm sure it hurts, but life goes on".

It certainly does – I wish you were wrong.

"Cheer up, he wouldn't want you to feel sad"

Cheer up, fuck off, are you mad?

Eight Years

8 years to stop my tears
And yet, they keep on falling

8 years to ease my pain
And yet, I am still bawling

8 years of missing you
Your love, your laughs, your way

8 years without your touch,
8 years this very day

I sometimes wonder where they've gone
The years spent without you

I've been living, like you said
Around my grief I grew

That doesn't mean it's easy though
8 years growing around grief

Living my life, in tribute to you
8 years of that belief

No Regrets

Not a day goes by when I don't think of your name.

Not a day goes by when I don't feel some pain.

Yet every day I live my life -

So thankful that I was your wife!

Every time I recall your face, your smile, your touch -

I know that I have been lucky to love so much.

No regrets, I embrace the pain.

And know that I would do it all again.

Thank You

Huge thanks to all the wonderful people I have in my life. Alive and dead! I really couldn't do this without you.

Thank you so much for buying and reading this book, without you my words would be written but unread! I would still be a writer, but perhaps not an author.

If you have the urge to write, please believe in yourself, if you want to be a writer, write. I would love to read some of your words so please get in touch or join my Facebook Group 'The Write Life with Claire'.

Claire is a stereotype smashing author, writing coach, reader, writer, and proud word-nerd. She is living her lifetime dream of being a writer. The opening paragraph to the story of her life would go something like this...

"Once upon a time there was a little girl who loved to read. She had a tricky time growing up but eventually became a teacher. Over 20 years she read many, many books to many, many children. With each book she read she dreamed of writing her own stories, stories to help little people believe that they can be who they want to be."

Claire made this dream come true and now writes books for children and adults. Her first book, The Princess Without a Crown, was published in 2020 and spent some time at Number 1 on Amazon for its genre, making her a Number 1 bestselling author! Her second book, The Pink Widow, was published in 2021 and shares her experiences of grief after becoming a widow in 2015.

As an author, and a writing coach, Claire spends her time writing and encouraging others to write and fulfil their writing dreams.

Facebook: @Claire Walsh Author @The Pink Widow

Instagram: @Out of the Box Books @The Pink Widow

TikTok @Claire.Walsh.Author

www.ootb-books.co.uk

outoftheboxbooks2020@gmail.com

Printed in Great Britain
by Amazon

32622762R10030